To: _____

From: _____

A HOME *Full of* GRACE

John & Susan Yates *and* Family

Baker Books

A Division of Baker Book House Co
Grand Rapids, Michigan 49516

© 2002 by John and Susan Yates
© 2002 Angus Hudson Ltd/Tim Dowley and Peter Wyart trading as Three's Company

Published under license in the USA by Baker Books
a division of Baker Book House Company
P.O. Box 6287, Grand Rapids, MI 49516-6287

Worldwide co-edition arranged and produced by Angus Hudson Ltd,
Concorde House, Grenville Place, Mill Hill, London NW7 3SA, England.
Tel: +44 (0) 20 8959 3668   Fax: +44 (0) 20 8959 3678

Printed in Singapore

Library of Congress Cataloging-in-Publication Data

Yates, John C., 1951–
    A home full of grace / John and Susan Yates.
            p.   cm.
    ISBN 0-8010-1241-4 (cloth)
    1. Family—Religious life. 2. Family—Religious aspects—
Christianity. I. Yates, Susan Alexander. II. Title.
BV4526.3 .Y38 2002
248.4—dc21   2002001932

Unless otherwise indicated, Scripture quotations are taken from the HOLY BIBLE, NEW INTERNATIONAL VERSION®. NIV®. Copyright © 1973, 1978, 1984 by International Bible Society. Used by permission of Zondervan. All rights reserved.

Cover photo © 2002 Nicholas DeVore/Stone.

Cover design by Cheryl Van Andel and Robin Black. Interior design by Robin Black.

Scripture quotations identified KJV are from the King James Version of the Bible.

For current information about all releases from Baker Book House, visit our web site:
                            http://www.bakerbooks.com

CONTENTS

family

Where two or more
persons are bound together
by marriage, by blood,
or by adoption,
you have family.

ONE

WHAT IS
A CHRISTIAN FAMILY?
John

From creation God intended that all people belong to a family. Marriage, home life, the nurture of children—these relationships and responsibilities are at the heart of God's original design. Where two or more persons are bound together by marriage, blood, or adoption, you have family.

In describing Eve as Adam's "helper" Scripture used a wonderful word that means the wife is an equal partner to the husband, essential in the accomplishment of God's purposes. The husband and wife need to support, encourage, and balance out each other.

We can learn how to nurture a strong marriage and family life. The principles are simple—they are rooted in Scripture and common sense. We need God's help as well as the encouragement and modeling of others to put them into practice.

EXPRESSIONS OF FAMILY

The Nuclear Family

Most Westerners think of family as a husband and wife or a mother, father, and child. From Genesis to Revelation, families—nuclear families—figure prominently in God's purposes. Our attention in this book focuses on this concept of family.

The Extended Family

The Old Testament sees families primarily as the broader family—grandparents, aunts, uncles, and cousins. I may have an aunt or a cousin I'm not anxious to claim, but regardless, they are part of my family and I have a responsibility to them.

The Church Family

Jesus greatly expanded our sense of family when he said that anyone who does the will of his heavenly Father is a mother or brother or sister to him (Matt. 12:46–30). My neighbor Bill is also my brother because he knows and loves Jesus Christ. We are brothers in Christ, and his son is "family" to me because he is part of the family of Christ.

WHAT IS A CHRISTIAN FAMILY?

A Christian family has consciously chosen to follow Jesus Christ, believing him to be the Son of God and Lord of the universe. It is not made up of perfect people. It is not immune to problems. It may face sickness, sadness, poverty, and great needs. The difference is that Christ is at work and honored in the home.

Our values are determined by God's eternal values instead of society's values.

In this family, the home becomes a place in which Christ would be pleased to dwell. There is prayer, forgiveness, faith, and joy.

Finally, the Christian family is part of the larger Christian community, the church. The family that seeks to be faithful to Christ apart from the church will find the going quite difficult. If you've not yet found a good church to belong to, ask God to lead you and begin seeking one now.

11

What Is *Different* about a Christian Home?

Christian home life differs radically from families where love for God and his Word are not central. Where homes are built upon Christ, three characteristics provide a sense of perspective and security.

No problem need overwhelm us when the Son of God is near.

We Live in the Light of Eternity

God is eternal and promises eternal life to those who believe in him. The temporary things of this life, which loom so large on our horizons, are not so important as they seem. Our values are determined by God's eternal values instead of society's values.

Realizing that one's child or one's mate is an eternal being gives a greater sense of appreciation, patience, and value. We do not expect perfection now, for we are all children, just beginning life from God's perspective. This equalizes us, it humbles us, it encourages us, it gives us a sense of the long view.

We Are Not Alone

Jesus taught that wherever two or three are gathered together in his name, he is in the midst of them through the presence of his Holy Spirit.

God is involved in every aspect of our life together. The Holy Spirit has taken up residence in every believer and, therefore, no believer is alone. We are linked spiritually in the family as well as linked by blood.

When Jesus walked the earth, his presence in a home brought such a sense of hopefulness that no sickness or sorrow could defeat those with whom he was present. No problem need overwhelm us when the Son of God is near. He can still calm a storm. He can still bring peace into a troubled room.

Prayer becomes crucial—it draws the family into unity. We are never dependent only upon our own resources but always may draw upon the limitless resources of our Father.

Jesus Christ, by his Spirit, dwells within us. This radically transforms our relationships. My son becomes also my brother in Christ. If I am impatient with him, in a sense I have been rude to Christ. If I lash out in anger and turn away from my mate, I am, in a sense, turning away from Christ himself. This mysterious truth of the presence of Christ gives us a new sense of holiness and wonder about our life together.

We Live in the Spirit of Grace

Perhaps the most precious word to the Christian is *grace*, which means God's free and unmerited favor. God not only forgives us our sins, but he gives us many wonderful gifts that we could never deserve.

In the home full of grace, forgiveness is always offered. The New Testament calls us to "be kind and compassionate to one another, forgiving each other, just as in Christ God forgave you" (Eph. 4:32). True reconciliation cannot occur apart from repentance, but we do not withdraw our love even if the one who offended us has not apologized. Resentment will eat a family up if it is not replaced by forgiveness.

There is a difficult balance here because tough love is sometimes needed. We don't want to be enablers of sin or harmful habits, but at the same time, we must always be forgiving, seeking to draw out the best in one another.

In a Christian home, courtesy and manners, kindness and patience are valued because they speak of grace. A home full of grace avoids negative words and attitudes because we know that all are made in the image of God. It is a safe place to fail and to learn.

Courtesy and manners, kindness and patience are valued because they speak of grace.

covenant

A marriage covenant is
a solemn, sacred, and
permanent commitment
made before God
by a man and a woman.

TWO

THREE ESSENTIAL COMMITMENTS FOR BUILDING THE CHRISTIAN HOME

John with Susan

Three basic commitments are foundational to building the Christian home—commitment to the *covenant*, to *communication*, and to *cultivating a vision*.

17

COMMITMENT TO THE COVENANT

At the heart of the Christian family is the marriage covenant, which God established at creation. A marriage covenant is a solemn, sacred, and permanent commitment made before God by a man and a woman. Because God has called us into covenant with himself through Christ, he never stops loving us or giving to us. We follow his example by honoring our marriage and being faithful to our mate. Like a strong fortress surrounding us and our children, the marriage covenant keeps us from pulling away from each other.

The marriage covenant builds security and forces us to deal with our problems.

The demands and temptations of busy careers may challenge the marriage covenant. Many married persons believe that their own personal growth and development must take precedence over their marriage commitment. But Christian men and women who marry must remember that the marriage covenant is the most solemn and sacred earthly commitment they will ever make, and they must make a permanent commitment to it. If marital difficulties threaten a relationship, but the husband and wife are committed to their covenant and dedicated to seeking help, they can rebuild their marriage. God always helps rebuild broken homes.

The marriage covenant builds security and forces us to deal with our problems. Martin Luther described marriage as a school for

18

character. Nothing reveals the cracks or strengths in one's character more quickly than the strains of married life, but, with the exception of the parent-child relationship, no other relationship has such potential to mature us.

Parental commitment to the marriage covenant also provides security for children and helps them know that despite disagreements, their parents' bond is permanent. Many children are plagued by the fear that their parents might divorce. By frequently asserting that they are married for keeps, parents can give their children the security they desperately need.

COMMITMENT TO COMMUNICATION

In most cases, family breakdown can be traced to communication breakdown. When conflict comes to a marriage, we are tempted to pull back from each other, nurse our own hurt feelings, and wait for the other to apologize. This can lead to *emotional divorce*, two people living under the same roof but unconnected. Although sometimes painful, the path to a deep, fulfilling marriage depends on persistent communication. It often involves deciding *again and again* not to give in to the temptation to isolation but instead working together through the hard times.

A wise couple makes time to sit and listen to each other every day, talking not only about the events of the day but also about their feelings and deeper concerns. Time for intimate conversation must be a priority.

COMMITMENT TO CULTIVATING A VISION

Cultivating a vision for your family is a third foundational commitment. The purpose of this book is to help you cultivate a vision and gain some tools for how to achieve that vision in your own home.

Married couples can dream about the family they want to establish and decide what values, priorities, and disciplines they will teach their children. While God intends for all families to be characterized by love, nurturing, and encouragement, your personal vision will determine the unique shape of your family.

The interests and abilities God has given you will guide your vision, and as you observe the character and talents of your children, you will know how to encourage their growth. As parents dream together about the future of their family, they will have a sense of mission and hope. This is their family vision.

Commitment to your marriage covenant, to communication within your home, and to cultivating a vision for your family early on in your married life provides an essential foundation for a strong family.

Time for intimate conversation must be a priority.

equipping

As our King, God helps us mature in character, faith, and godliness, equipping us for our roles of marriage partner and parent.

THREE

ESTABLISHING A STRONG MARRIAGE
John with Susan

THE FOUNDATION

If we desire to establish a strong marriage, our first priority must be our relationship with God. Jesus said the foremost commandment is "Love the Lord your God with all your heart, and with all your soul, and with all your mind" (Matt. 22:37). As important as our relationship with our spouse is, it is secondary to our relationship to our Lord, who wants our whole heart.

In the Sermon on the Mount, the Lord stressed that our first priority is to seek the kingdom of God and his righteousness (Matt. 6:33). To seek the kingdom of God means simply to let God be King of our life. Then we will experience humility and a deep desire to obey him. As our King, God helps us mature in character, faith, and godliness, equipping us for our roles of marriage partner and parent.

Our mate is our most important earthly friend.

Before God can become King of my life, I must believe that Christ is the Son of God and desire to know him better, acknowledging my failure to be all God wants me to be and asking for forgiveness. And I must ask God to be the center of my life. I learn to pray and let him speak to me through the Scriptures and through the Holy Spirit. As my relationship with him deepens, my life begins to change, and I learn to entrust myself to God.

Our next priority must be our relationship with our spouse. Genesis 2:18–24 describes how God created for man a perfectly matched companion, and the two became deeply committed to each other. Later on, God gave the couple children. We are alone together as man and wife first before our children come, and then later, after they grow up and depart, we are alone together again. Our mate is our most important earthly friend. If we value our relationship, it will remain strong.

FIVE BASIC LESSONS

Every Christian couple must learn at least *five basic lessons* to build a strong marriage.

1. *Some of your expectations for the marriage will conflict with your mate's expectations.* To build a strong, loving relationship, couples must learn early on to express their hopes and expectations and to accept those of their spouse, though they may be very different.

2. *Valuing your differences is crucially important.* When we talk about our differences, we grow to better understand and appreciate each other.

3. *Couples need to learn to maintain romance in their relationship.* A husband must remember to focus on his wife and not take her for granted. Similarly, the wife is to live with her husband's needs and desires uppermost in her mind. (Read Paul's teaching in Eph. 5:21–33.)

4. *Most married couples need to learn the importance of simply being together and talking regularly.* A meaningful romantic relationship depends on frequent, in-depth times of communication. When we lose touch with our mate's interests and goals, our relationship is weakened and often breaks.

5. *Husbands and wives need a shared faith in God.* A complete marriage is not simply a horizontal relationship; it is more like a triangle, with the husband and wife both growing vertically in their relationship with God. Few of us are strong enough to maintain a solid marriage today apart from God's help. By praying together, discussing

God's Word, and attending church together, a couple strengthens their bond with each other and with God.

The Book of Ecclesiastes pictures this relationship in these lovely words:

> Two are better than one,
>   because they have a good return for their work:
> If one falls down,
>   his friend can help him up.
> But pity the man who falls
>   and has no one to help him up!
> Also, if two lie down together, they will keep warm.
>   But how can one keep warm alone?
> Though one may be overpowered,
>   two can defend themselves.
> A cord of three strands is not quickly broken.

Ecclesiastes 4:9–12

This is a picture of a marriage in Christ. The threefold strand is a husband and wife whose lives have been intertwined with the life of God.

control

Wherever you are in life,
God is in control.

FOUR

The Seasons of Family Life

Susan

We all go through different seasons in life, some much more difficult than others, but all full of great challenges and significant rewards if we have the eyes to see them.

In each season we are likely to experience frustrations, and it may seem as though we're struggling alone in a season that will never end. When the season passes and we look back, however, we realize that many of the things that seemed so crucial really weren't. It is helpful to have the counsel of friends who are older and have lived through a few more seasons than we have.

THE EARLY YEARS TOGETHER

The first few years of marriage can be awkward, and they can be delightful. A couple needs a sense of humor during this season as they learn to live with differences and discover how they can become one.

When the first baby arrives, we enter a new season overnight, and we wonder how one small being can cause so many immediate changes.

Of course the joy of this season is indescribable as we hold our babies and gain a whole new understanding of how God our Father adores us. Our love for our children is a wonderful taste of what God's love for us must be like.

RAISING CHILDREN

For parents, the toddler years are the most trying and the most precious. Energetic children are exhausting, and yet they also delight us with their unpredictability.

During our children's school years, we face new and different challenges that can be emotionally exhausting. Children have different needs, and it's easy to feel overwhelmed as we attempt to meet them. Wise parents stay close to their children, carefully listening and observing.

Our love for our children is a wonderful taste of what God's love for us must be like.

When children are teenagers and facing the problems of adolescence, parents must teach them to pray about decisions they must make and to take their loneliness and sadness to God and find companionship with him.

John and I personally feel that it is best for a mother to be at home when the children are small and in school. It makes a big difference if Mom is there to listen and comfort, to carpool, and to be a friend. It is certainly not always possible, but the more it can be done, the better.

31

BEING ALONE AGAIN

From the time the children are small, parents need to be preparing themselves for when their children will leave. This will make the adjustment to the empty nest much easier. Once the children are grown, parents have the freedom to choose options they have not had before, and this is a time to pursue, as individuals and as couples, interests they have postponed. This is also a time for the benefits of solitude.

Wise parents stay close to their children, carefully listening and observing.

Wherever we are in life, God is in control. He is our rock and our fortress (Ps. 31:2–3), always ready to lead and guide us. Sometimes we have to turn away from the challenges at hand and simply look to God for comfort and peace. He has a purpose and plan for every phase of our life, and he is the master of what happens. He has called us to be exactly where we are, promising, "I will instruct you and teach you in the way you should go; I will counsel you and watch over you" (Ps. 32:8). Ask God to teach you in this season you are in right now. Come to him with hopeful expectancy, looking to learn from him in each season of life.

children

Children are a gift from the Lord that may come later, but family begins with just two people.

FIVE

THE FIRST CHILD
Allison with Will

A s young couples begin their life journey together, there are issues relating to parenthood they must discuss. Family planning is one of the most obvious. It is important to agree on what measures will be taken so that children will come when the couple is ready for them.

Ultimately, of course, our having children is up to God. He is in control, and we must surrender to his lordship. We can have confidence that God knows what is best.

We must also have a clear understanding of what it means to be a family. In the eyes of God, a husband and wife bound together in the Holy Spirit make the family unit whole. Children are a gift from the Lord that may come later, but family begins with just two people. Understanding this concept of a family is essential, because a solid foundational relationship between husband and wife makes functioning as godly parents possible.

ISSUES TO CONSIDER

When thinking of having children, a couple should consider the following:

1. *You will never be completely ready.* You will never be smart enough, rich enough, or experienced enough to have children. You have to learn as you go.

2. *Give yourselves time to cleave together as man and wife before you have children.*

3. *Learn to develop and stick to a family budget.* This is not to say that you must wait until you "have enough money" before you have a child, but it is advisable to be as debt-free as possible.

4. *Talk about it!* Understand what your mate thinks about having children. If you or your spouse has a history of divorce, unfaithfulness, alcoholism, or abuse in your family of origin, seek godly counseling to prepare you for having children of your own.

5. *Who are your role models in parenting?* Your own parents may be godly models, but if you or your spouse grew up in a home you do not want to emulate, it is crucial that you

Pray for God's direction about when to have children.

spend time with Christian families you admire. Ask questions about parenting and discipline methods.

6. *Pray.* We should commit every aspect of our lives to prayer. Pray for God's direction about when to have children. Pray for agreement between you and your spouse.

7. *Trust that God knows best.* He will walk with you through the trials, for he promised, "I will never leave you nor forsake you" (Josh. 1:5).

THE CHANGES OF PREGNANCY

It would take an entire book to describe the changes that pregnancy brings to a woman *and* to a man. Men do not become pregnant, but they do go through many emotional changes. Discuss with your obstetrician, as well as with close friends who have had children, the changes you can expect during pregnancy. It is encouraging to understand what is happening, and it is reassuring to know that others have experienced the same highs and lows as you.

37

The most obvious changes during pregnancy are the physical changes to the woman's body. Along with the physical transformation come even more mystifying emotional changes. Many of these are linked to hormones; others simply are a woman's reaction to the physical changes in her body.

During this time the intimate relationship between husband and wife may become strained. Because a pregnant woman is often uncomfortable with her changing body, she may not want to make love with her husband. Often hormonal shifts decrease a woman's libido during pregnancy. In some cases, though, these same hormones cause an increase in sexual fervor. This may be a wonderful thing—or an awkward thing—as a husband's desire for his wife may change as he sees her body change. He may worry that sexual intimacy will hurt the baby or his wife (in all but the rarest cases it will not), and he may be unsure of how to express his physical desire.

Let each other know your feelings about the changes pregnancy causes, and pray together—for yourselves and for your child. Husbands, be careful to express to your wife how much you love her and her changing figure! Wives, have patience with your man, as he truly cannot understand what is happening to you. The intimacy and unity you developed before pregnancy will help you be patient with each other's concerns.

Read Psalm 139 and rejoice in the miracle that God is doing.

> *The intimacy and unity you developed before pregnancy will help you be patient with each other's concerns.*

AFTER THE BABY ARRIVES

Children of Christian parents are children of the covenant, and they belong to the Lord in a special way. We know that God loves and cares for them perfectly, more than we in our weakness are able. He will fill in the gaps when our parenting is imperfect. When our children misbehave, we need not be devastated, or when they excel, we do not take all the credit, because they belong to the Lord. We are simply stewards of our children for a short time.

mothers

We will not be
the mothers we want to be
apart from God.

SIX

MOTHERHOOD
Susan

A mother bonds with her child from the moment of conception, and the cutting of the umbilical cord in no way severs the deep emotional and spiritual union. With a unique ability to nurse and nurture her baby, a mother has a different and more intense need to be close to her child than a father has. While a mother's love for her child may not be any greater than the father's love, God gives a mother a tender, alert sensitivity to her child and a fiercely protective instinct that the father often does not completely understand.

When it comes to training, teaching, or guiding the children, both mother and father must accept the responsibility. Today some fathers are home more than used to be the custom, and surely this is a good thing. Fathers can be nurturers too. Mothers and fathers parent as a team, each bearing equal responsibility for their children.

Still, even with the support of our husband, we will not be the mothers we want to be apart from God. We need to make time alone with God the first priority of the day, praying and claiming the promises in Scripture. My quiet times have been my lifeline, because each day I learn in a fresh way how much I need God and how faithfully he is with me.

FINDING SOME GIRLFRIENDS

Seldom does a mother of small children have a sense of accomplishment or appreciation. If you are a mother of small children, you need the companionship of other moms in the same season of parenting—moms who will encourage and pray for you and with whom you can trade child care or go to the park. Another mother can empathize with your frustration and appreciate the monotony of your daily routine. You also need friends who are older than you are, who can speak to you from their experience.

Female role models encourage us and also mentor us. Especially if you come from a broken or dysfunctional home, having an older friend to guide you is a tremendous help. And we must also be willing to be that older friend in some young mother's life. Titus 2:4 calls older women to "train the younger women to love their husbands and children."

Female role models encourage us and also mentor us.

KEEPING YOUR HUSBAND FIRST

It is all too easy for a young mother to assume that she will work on her marriage when things calm down. But things don't calm down. Life only gets more complicated, and responsibilities and options increase. In our child-centered world we must be careful not to put our marriage on hold. If we invest all of our energy in our children, we may find, when the children leave home, that we have a shallow relationship with our spouse. When children see us putting our husband first, they see lived out in our lives a radical biblical truth—the primacy of the marital relationship.

43

God's Family

Motherhood is a high and holy calling. There is no greater privilege than being a nurturer. But what does this mean practically speaking? Children need our time, both quality and quantity. Young children need little blocks of time with Mom for doing things together. A teenager may need an unscheduled extended time to discuss a problem. Part of nurturing is being available. It makes children feel valuable.

Proverbs 27:23 says, "Be sure you know the condition of your flocks, give careful attention to your herds." I have taken this passage as encouragement to study my children. I pray, "God, give me sharp antennae that can discern the needs of this child." One of the special gifts God gives mothers is a sensitivity to their child's heart. Because mothers are often with their children, they are aware of needs as they arise. Our privilege is to introduce our children to the daily reality of a relationship with Christ. While walking through daily routines, take advantage of opportunities to pray with your children.

As a mother I have found it helpful to remind myself that God gives to each of us exactly the children we need through adoption or through birth, in the correct birth order, and with their unique natures. He gives us these children not only for us to nurture, but also as his tools in our lives to help us grow into the women he created us to be. Every child is a gift from God, and God will use each one in a special way to nurture us in our relationship with him.

One of the special gifts God gives mothers is a sensitivity to their child's heart.

dependent

To manage his home
effectively, a man must
learn to be prayerfully
dependent on God.

SEVEN

FATHERHOOD
John

E very father has three roles—*manager, minister,* and *model*. By filling these roles, a man takes responsibility for his family and assures that their material, emotional, intellectual, social, and spiritual needs are met.

MANAGER

In describing qualities that make a man worthy of leadership in the church, Paul wrote, "He must manage his own family well and see that his children obey him with proper respect" (1 Tim. 3:4). A father can't manage very effectively from a distance; he needs to be intimately

involved with his family. Most fathers actually spend less time with their children than they think they do. When young children, who are extremely vulnerable, spend hours in front of the TV and only minutes with Dad, it's easy to discern how their values will be formed. Time with our children must be a priority.

Every father needs wisdom, and none of us starts out wise—wisdom must be learned. We learn from experiences with our children and from other dads, so talk to other men and learn from them.

To manage his home effectively, a man must learn to be prayerfully dependent on God. Ask God for his help and pray about the kind of dad you want to be—patient, available, wise, and understanding.

It is worth whatever it takes to get the message of love across.

MINISTER

If we don't shepherd our children, who will? They always need it, no matter how old they are. We do this by being sensitive to their needs and doing things with them. Young children need our involvement in their lives in small segments of time, but as they get older they need larger blocks of our time.

Our children depend on us to be sure their needs are being met, and they often need to hear us tell them that we love them. Sometimes it's difficult for a dad to speak openly and tenderly of his love for his children, but they need this more than anything else. Plan to tell them often, think about what to say, be willing to be vulnerable. It is worth whatever it takes to get the message of love across.

MODEL

A Christian man is shaped by his relationship with God, and only the two of them know just how genuine it is. A wise man will ask God to reveal to him those areas in which he needs to grow and mature as well as those sins of which he needs to repent. The strength of a man lies in the depth of his relationship with his Creator.

A Christian father has the responsibility to teach God's truths to his children and grandchildren to the best of his ability. If he is wise, he will use whatever opportunities arise to help them understand how biblical principles apply to daily life. If the Bible is important to Dad, it will be honored by the whole family.

If the Bible is important to Dad, it will be honored by the whole family.

God gave this instruction: "These commandments that I give you today are to be upon your hearts. Impress them on your children. Talk about them when you sit at home and when you walk along the road, when you lie down and when you get up" (Deut. 6:6–7). In other words, we are to use daily opportunities to teach the practical implications of the Word of God.

50

You may not have been trained in the Scriptures as a child, and you can't teach what you don't know. That's why the most important discipline in your life will be taking time each day for Bible reading and prayer.

Don't give up on your goal to be the best father you can possibly be. Choose to be strong, persevering, and faithful. God will help you if you choose to be mature and to walk in his ways.

security

When children understand that family members are totally accepted simply because they are family, they gain a sense of peace and security.

EIGHT

THE ATMOSPHERE
IN A CHRISTIAN HOME
Susan

Paul says that followers of Christ spread a "fragrance" or "sweet aroma" through which God manifests himself wherever we go (2 Cor. 2:14–16). This aroma of Christ is what we want for our homes. As we parents live in Christ, he enables us to bear the fruit of his Spirit: love, joy, peace, patience, kindness, goodness, faithfulness, gentleness, and self-control (Gal. 5:22–23). Through these fruit our home becomes a place of love, forgiveness, and joy.

AN ATMOSPHERE OF LOVE

Developing an atmosphere that radiates love in the home requires our acceptance of God's unconditional love for us. Christ says to those who follow him, "As the Father has loved me, so have I loved you" (John 15:9). And the apostle Paul wrote, "God demonstrates his own love for us in this: While we were yet sinners, Christ died for us" (Rom. 5:8). Nothing we do or don't do can change his love for us.

When the love of God flows from us into our homes, they will be places of sacrifice, acceptance, and appreciation. We cannot have love without sacrifice. Children must be taught to serve each other as an offering to God. From a very young age, they can participate in chores and they can learn to do things for others without being asked. The family that develops sacrificial service will be a family where love is practiced.

The Christian home should provide the security of acceptance—a place where we are seen as valuable and loved people simply because God made us and loves us. When we are confident that God accepts us, we find it easier to accept and support others. One way we do this is by expressing appreciation for one another's good qualities. Husbands and wives need to express appreciation and gratitude to each other in front of their children. And they need to recognize their children's unique God-given qualities. Applaud them and let them know you delight in all that is special about them.

When children understand that family members are totally accepted simply because they are family, they gain a sense of peace and security. Knowing that our parents love us this way helps us to understand God's acceptance and love for us as well.

The family that develops sacrificial service will be a family where love is practiced.

An Atmosphere of Forgiveness

Forgiveness enables tension to be released and peace to return to our homes. Unless forgiveness flows freely, bitterness and resentment take hold. Practicing forgiveness is difficult, however, unless we have first accepted God's readily available and abundant forgiveness of us. Grateful for Christ's death on the cross as payment for our sins, we humbly go to God, confidently asking him to forgive us. As we experience this in our own lives, we are able to forgive others.

We often do not *feel* like forgiving our mate or our children, but forgiveness has nothing to do with feelings. We forgive because God has told us to forgive, and forgiveness must occur before healing can take place. When forgiveness is offered, healing begins and feelings slowly start to change.

Praise and thanksgiving to God produce within us a spirit of joy.

An Atmosphere of Joy

Supernatural joy grows out of our relationship with the Lord. It is the second fruit of the Spirit (Gal. 5:22) and is distinct from happiness. Happiness is usually caused by circumstances. We feel happy when things are going well but feel down or depressed when life is not going well. Supernatural joy, however, grows out of a sense that we are resting in God's loving arms whatever our circumstances might be. We do not always feel

happy, but we can always have a deep sense of joy that we belong to God and that his plans for us are good. Joy is his gift to us, and it refreshes us. Praise and thanksgiving to God produce within us a spirit of joy.

Children who grow up in an atmosphere of love, forgiveness, and joy will be emotionally and spiritually healthy. They will be secure and will know how to build loving homes themselves. God will work with us to create this loving atmosphere. Indeed, this is his plan.

character

*A living relationship
with God that produces
Christian character
will sustain a child and
an adult and a family.*

NINE

BUILDING CHRISTIAN CHARACTER

John

Some parents seem to think that their goal as parents is to make sure their children are always happy. Therefore, they tend to give their children whatever they want and say yes to most of their requests. They are, in fact, ensuring the eventual unhappiness of their children, for sooner or later everyone learns that life does not always bring us happiness. Life brings disappointments, painful challenges, temptations, and setbacks. Our job as Christian parents is to do all we can to ensure that our children have the endurance and stamina, the courage and dedication to carry on in the face of adversity and

to be men and women of integrity no matter what. A living relationship with God that produces Christian character will sustain a child and an adult and a family.

TRAINING IN CHARACTER

We work to raise young people who have a clear sense of who they are, what they believe, what they stand for, what they stand against, and where they are going. They must get this from their parents, and we cannot give it to them unless we have it ourselves. All our lives we too must be growing in Christian character.

Children do not just evolve naturally into godly people on their own. As parents we need to determine what character qualities are most important and work at communicating them to our children from the time they are very young. Our job is to equip our children for life, and training them in character development is the soul of this responsibility.

Parents must help their children make the wisest and best choices and guide them into godliness. Children are like clay—they are pliable, and we are able to shape their moral character. Television, the media, and the cinema will not train our children to be charitable, patient, compassionate, and chaste. We must show our children the way and pray that they will indeed embrace godliness.

If we continue growing ourselves, we can help our children to do the same.

GOD'S PERSPECTIVE ON CHARACTER

Character is of the greatest concern to our Father in heaven. The God who gave us life and in whom we trust is the essence of pure goodness, and he wants his children to develop his character. God's Holy Spirit is even more concerned than we are about shaping our children's character, and he becomes our partner in the process. We must seek his guidance and learn to depend on him, trust him, and obey him. He will give us the wisdom to know how to help our children grow in goodness.

All of us are people in process, and it is God's intention that we parents be deepening our own moral character at the same time we are seeking to help our children become mature men and women. If we continue growing ourselves, we can help our children to do the same. Discuss often what matters most in being a person of godly character, and then live that way as your children's model. When you fail, honestly admit it.

We must have the highest expectations of ourselves and our children.

THE VALUE OF CHRISTIAN CHARACTER

Our culture does not share our Christian understanding of character. Many people seem to believe that success in life is simply getting what you want, and if you have to tell some lies and break some laws in the process, it doesn't make any difference. As followers of Jesus, however, our model is Christ himself, and the virtues that he taught and lived are those to which we are called. We must have the highest expectations of ourselves and our children.

At the heart of Christian character is integrity. Integrity is more than honesty; it involves trustworthiness, objectivity, fair-mindedness,

sincerity, and thoroughness. A person who lives with integrity lives by the highest standard—the principles set forth in God's Word.

Christian character also encompasses compassion, teachability, courage, self-discipline, and determination. Thoughtful parents will consider what character traits they want their children to develop. They will realize that their children will develop these qualities only to the degree that they see them lived out in their parents' lives. Teach them the highest standards and commit yourself to living up to those standards yourself. Expect the same of your kids, but be gentle and understanding when they fall short. None of us achieves perfection in this life.

parenting

God is the model
for good parenting—
high in support and
high in control.

TEN

DISCIPLINE IN THE HOME
John with Susan

Christian parents want to raise children who desire to obey God. The Bible says that God "disciplines us for our good, that we may share his holiness" (Heb. 12:10). So also a parent must discipline his child, but as he does, he should be asking himself, *How can I best help my child learn from this situation?* Ongoing discipline must be instructive, or the child will profit very little.

Discipline grows out of love. Without love, discipline becomes hard and cruel. But love without discipline is just sentimentality. When a parent has maintained a strong loving relationship with her child, situations that demand discipline will actually bring the parent and child closer together.

CONTROL AND SUPPORT

In the first four to six years of life, children learn to obey or to disobey. Waiting too long to expect obedience can be a mistake. Note what the Proverbs teach. "Folly is bound up in the heart of a child, but the rod of discipline will drive it far from him" (22:15).

God is the model for good parenting—high in support and high in control. Because of his love for us, he has laid down principles we need to follow if we're going to enjoy an abundant life. He brings about circumstances to discipline us when we fail to obey and turn away from his established ways. When parents are able to maintain control (the

ability to manage a child's behavior) and support (the ability to make a child feel loved) they are following God's model.

CARING DISCIPLINE

Hebrews 12:9 says, "We have all had human fathers who disciplined us and we respected them for it." If our children can understand that we discipline them because we love them, they will grow to appreciate the discipline we have given them. But they will not appreciate it at the time. We have to take the long-range view: What our children think of us now is not nearly as important as what they will think of us twenty years from now.

Ongoing discipline must be instructive, or the child will profit very little.

Whatever method of discipline we use, it is important to remember three things. First, we must let our children know what we expect—what is acceptable behavior. Second, we must be consistent. Third, we must always seek to reaffirm our love for the child in the midst of the discipline and make the misbehavior and resulting discipline a learning experience.

Parents need to present a united front, agreeing on what is right and wrong, what behavior is acceptable and unacceptable. Discuss the issues that may come up and decide on rules, expectations, and consequences.

Parents must communicate principles, not just rules. This is what Jesus did. When children are very small, we simply have to say this is right and that is wrong. But one of our greatest challenges as children grow up is to communicate clear moral principles to them.

As we focus on the behavior of our children, we must also be honest with them about our own personal struggles with self-discipline. We will let our children down if we imply that when we became an adult we no longer had problems with self-discipline. Because children need to understand this aspect of being an adult, it is important to tell them of some of our temptations and failures.

Every one of us must ultimately depend on the grace and mercy of God to get through life. If we can help our children understand this when they are young, they will have happier adult years.

Parents must learn to distinguish between honest mistakes and willful disobedience. When you tell your child to stay in her room and she goes out into the yard, that's disobedience. But when a child spills his milk at the table, that's a mistake. When a child is willfully disobedient, the consequences should be firm and swift, whereas the consequences of mistakes should be lenient and instructive.

BALANCE

Wise parents want to aim at a balance between saying yes and saying no to their children. Parents who are too strict create a stifling, negative atmosphere in the home and produce children who begin to feel they can't please their parents. But the children of parents who are too lenient will become self-centered, rude, and obnoxious.

We will make many mistakes in disciplining our children, particularly when we are tired or under stress. We are weak, fallible creatures, but we are in partnership with a great and mighty God. As we seek his help, he will enable our children to mature into fine men and women.

Wise parents want to aim at a balance between saying yes and saying no to their children.

nurturing

The responsibility of nurturing our children in the faith is largely ours, and the Lord Jesus will give us the wisdom to do it.

ELEVEN

CULTIVATING FAITH
Susan with John

When parents decide that in their family God will come first, they are in the process of building a Christian home. Even if one spouse is not at the place of being able to make this commitment, God will honor the parent who must take this step alone. However, the goal of having a Christian home will not be fully realized until both parents are committed to God's leadership.

LEADING OUR CHILDREN TO CHRIST

When children are very young, they can understand that God loves them and sent his Son Jesus Christ to show us how to live and to take away our sins on the cross.

Our children's hunger for God's Word will grow as they observe our hunger.

Each child must make the decision to invite Christ into his or her life to live there forever as friend and master. When children invite Christ in, the Holy Spirit takes residence and begins to work in their young hearts and continues to mold them into the people he has created them to be.

It is largely the parents' responsibility to nurture our children in the faith, and the Lord Jesus will give us the wisdom to do it. Therefore, family prayers, Bible study, and discussions about our lives as Christians must be integral parts of our children's growing up years.

A GROWING DEPENDENCE ON THE FATHER

As we raise our children in the Christian faith, our goal as parents must be to steadily turn our children from dependence on us to dependence on their heavenly Father. Through God's provision of his Word, prayer, fellowship, vision, and worship, we learn to depend on him.

The Importance of God's Word

One of the greatest legacies we can pass on to our children is familiarity with the stories, promises, and principles found in the Bible. Wise parents will seek out Bible storybooks and will develop a discipline of reading Bible stories to their children.

Our children's hunger for God's Word will grow as they observe our hunger. If they see us spending time reading the Bible, they will be more likely as adolescents to initiate their own personal study. At a Christian bookstore, you will find devotional guides for children of all ages.

Prayer

The most effective way to teach our children the importance of prayer is to pray with them regularly. As we demonstrate to them the three basic ways God answers prayers—yes, no, wait—we can teach them that

God's answers are always best because of his great love for us. We should also encourage them to pray for others—neighbors, the community, the nation, and the world.

Fellowship

Christians need each other. The love and encouragement of close friends is vitally important to our personal growth and maturity. This may be especially true for children. Church youth groups and parachurch organizations pull kids together for fellowship, mission work, Bible study, and worship.

A Sense of Vision

Without playing God in their lives, parents can help their children develop a passion for a Christlike life and a vision for their own personal ministry. As God helps us see our children's potential, we encourage them and dream with them about the many ways in which God might use their gifts. We should not, however, try to determine their professions or vocations. God is the one who calls our children to the life he has designed for them.

Worship

Regular corporate worship with the church family is an important part of our life with God. When we make a priority of worship as a family, it communicates to our children that we are willing to set aside time to join with other believers in praising God. This tells our children how important Almighty God is and that we honor him.

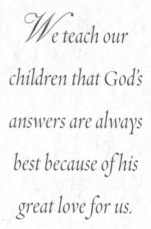

We teach our children that God's answers are always best because of his great love for us.

As we honestly share our own experience of God and our journey of faith with our children, we will be growing together in the knowledge of the goodness and greatness of God and in the awareness of our constant need for him in our lives.

becoming

Our children
are maturing,
weaning themselves
from us, and becoming
their own persons.

TWELVE

Parents and Adolescents
Susan

Teenagers, who are no longer children but not yet adults, often confuse themselves and everyone around them with their sudden mood shifts and attempts at expressing their individuality.

The Awkward Teen

Young people want very much to grow up physically, but the process can be frustrating. From their perspective, they develop either too early or too late. We have to help our young people understand that what is happening to their bodies is normal.

Teenagers are also frustrated because at times they want to be dependent children and at other times seek desperately to be independent and mature. Parents often feel like they are walking on eggshells when trying to anticipate what their adolescent child's needs and reactions will be.

Sometimes our children seem to be trying on different personality types to find the one that fits them best, because they're really not sure who they are. Friends help teens define who they are and are very important at this time.

Often adolescence is awkward spiritually as well. This is a time when children need to develop their own personal faith, separate from that of their parents. Parents need to be extremely patient and prayerful during this time.

Parents need to be extremely patient and prayerful during this time.

The Awkward Parent

As our young people begin to develop their own viewpoints we need to recognize that they are maturing, weaning themselves from us, and becoming their own persons. We wonder what is realistic to expect from them and what disciplines we should maintain.

Gifts You Can Give

When our children become teenagers, we have the opportunity of developing deep friendships with them. During this time, there are a number of gifts we can give them that will enhance these friendships.

Giving Them Time

Wise parents of teenagers try to be around their kids. They may plop down on their teenage daughter's bed and chat about her day or kick around a soccer ball with their son. Giving your child time is a way of saying, "I like you; I want to be with you."

Showing Them Respect

Asking for our teen's ideas about things communicates that we are interested in knowing what he thinks and that his perspective is valuable to us.

Telling our children repeatedly how grateful and proud we are to be their parents lets them know that we respect and admire them. Commenting on the positive balances out the necessary correcting that we must also do during the teen years.

Creating a Positive Attitude toward the Future

Frustration and disappointment crowd into teenagers' lives. Wise parents have to try to understand the agonizing impact of the disappointment but also convey trust in God to work things out. Romans 8:28 is a wonderful promise to claim during difficult times.

Appreciating Their Friends

Wise parents of teenagers try to be around their kids.

Parents are wise to create the kind of home atmosphere that encourages their children to bring their friends home. Think of things you can do to make your home a fun place for your children and their peers. Have plenty of good food on hand, because teenagers are always hungry.

Sometimes you may find that you do not like your child's friend, and you must be careful here. It can be tricky telling your teen of your concerns about a certain friend. Discuss this with a counselor, teacher, or another more experienced adult.

Giving Your Children Parameters

Teenagers need parameters, but they must gradually have fewer rules and increasing freedom to make their own decisions to prepare for adulthood. As teenagers express their independence in various ways, we have to have wisdom about what to allow.

Mom and Dad need to agree on what the crucial issues are in the family and explain these things clearly and consistently to the kids. Teenagers need to hear the "why" of family policies and not just the "what."

Giving Your Children Other Adult Friends

One of the greatest gifts we can give our children is the privilege of sharing in friendships with our close adult friends. Friendships with adults other than one's parents are extremely important in providing models and counsel for our young people.

Teenagers make us realize how imperfect we are as parents. Remember that there is no mistake God cannot rectify, no crisis he cannot redeem.

alongside

When children are young
adults, parenthood
becomes a walking
alongside rather than a
pulling from the front or
pushing from behind.

THIRTEEN

Preparing Your Child
for Independence
John III with Siblings

The greatest gifts a parent can give a child are a love for God's Word and a passion for prayer. Preparing a child for independence starts with the sharing of responsibility and the expectation that he will be trustworthy. A child who has been trusted and has over time proved trustworthy will be much better able to make wise decisions once he is away from home. It will also be much easier for the parents to let their child go.

83

INCREASING SUPPORT

More often than not, young people are far more eager to leave home than their parents are to see them go. At this point, for good or ill, phys-

ical control over your children becomes impossible. Your options then are threefold. You could try to exert long-distance control through phone calls, e-mails, and letters; you could gratefully wash your hands of the responsibility of exercising any control at all; or you could seek to redefine what sort of control, in conjunction with support, is now appropriate. This third option, though the hardest, is clearly the best.

When your ability to control is limited, offering wise support is an excellent alternative. Be interested in what your child is doing, ask about her new friends, but don't try to get too much information. Ask few questions and listen a lot.

One of the best ways my parents showed support for me was by writing periodic letters. Getting mail, any mail, is a great thing; and to a young person sensitive about his or her independence, it is less intrusive than a phone call.

Acceptable Control

With the many temptations that come with independence, young people are bound to mess up in some way. Unwise behavior shouldn't be condoned, but neither should parents dwell on it. Wise parents will let a child know how they feel and leave it at that.

Showing a disregard for the law or for important family principles, however, is unacceptable. In these cases parents must take a stand. Young adults will need boundaries set for them if they fail to set their own.

One area where parents will most certainly be challenged and will need to be firm is money. University students especially will never have enough and will often come to their parents for more.

Laying down guidelines before a child goes off to college is the best way to forestall major problems. A good maxim to follow is: Let young adults make mistakes as long as they continue to learn from them. When

When your ability to control is limited, offering wise support is an excellent alternative.

85

they fail to learn from their mistakes or are put in danger because of them, it is time to intervene.

Sharing prayer requests and enlisting their prayer support communicates respect that all children desire.

BUILDING A FRIENDSHIP

For a young adult nothing is more affirming than being treated as a peer by their parents and their parents' friends. Being invited to join conversations, being asked his or her opinion, and being treated like an adult all go a long way toward helping a young person mature. At this point parenthood becomes a walking alongside rather than a pulling from the front or pushing from behind. Of course, such a friendship will not grow and deepen without effort on the part of both the child and the parents.

One natural way to help your friendship with adult children grow deeper is to let them be involved in the decision making and dreaming that go on in midlife and later. As you have sought to be involved in their lives, seek to involve them in yours. By asking advice and seeking the input of your children, you demonstrate high levels of trust and respect, which young adults relish. One easy way to do this is by asking your children—of all ages—to pray for you. Sharing prayer

requests and enlisting their prayer support communicates respect that all children desire.

This time of transition from dependence to independence can be stressful for both children and parents. Parents will often feel like coaches standing on the sidelines shouting themselves hoarse only to be ignored by the players on the field. For kids it often feels like having a persistent backseat driver distracting you as you negotiate new and often treacherous roads. Thankfully, this time of stress and miscommunication doesn't last forever. With continued support and involvement in each other's lives, the path is paved for true and lasting friendships.

privilege

Prayer is at the heart
of friendship with God,
and prayer for our families
is our responsibility
and our privilege.

FOURTEEN

PRAYING
FOR YOUR FAMILY
John

Though prayer may not come easily, we need to embrace our responsibility, for prayer is at the heart of effective parenting. We refer to this as a part of the parents' priestly role in the home.

GETTING THE MOST OUT OF PRAYER

The apostle Paul says that we should pray at all times, but we will never learn to pray at all times unless we learn to pray at certain times.

So establish a time and attempt to preserve that time every day. Then decide on a place where you can be still and quiet without interruptions. Realize that God is in that place, wherever it is, and therefore it is a holy place.

Begin by thanking God. Take a moment or two to look back over the past few days and give God thanks for the blessings that come to your

mind. If you begin the day with thankfulness, it will give you a sense of joy and peace.

Think over the past twenty-four hours and ask God to help you remember what happened. As you review the day, take to God anything you think of that is significant, asking him to help you profit from yesterday.

Consider today's concerns. Maybe you will pull out your daily calendar and look at appointments or plans. Pray about these things one by one, asking God to help you be adequate for the challenges you face during the day. Ask him to fill you with his Holy Spirit and make you joyful.

If you begin the day with thankfulness, it will give you a sense of joy and peace.

PRAYING PARENTS

A Canaanite woman who had a demon-possessed daughter once approached Jesus on her daughter's behalf. She came to Jesus at a time when he was trying to have a little privacy. He seemed to ignore her. Perhaps he was seeking to teach his disciples something at that moment. She, however, persisted in imploring him. Finally, in his own time, he responded by meeting the little girl's need.

This woman shows us a good deal about praying for our family. She comes to God through Christ, and so must we, for he is our mediator.

91

She acknowledges her need, coming in humility, and she tells Jesus specifically what her needs are. She makes careful, clear requests. Finally, she is persistent. She does not lose heart. She is a good model for us as praying parents.

It helps when praying for loved ones to envision them before Jesus Christ. Jesus was unfailingly compassionate when people came to him with needs. As you pray for your family, bring them one by one before the Lord, thanking him for their good qualities and interceding on behalf of their needs.

We can make a difference in the future generations if we start praying now.

You may be saying to yourself, *I'm not sure I know how to pray or what to include in my prayers. Maybe I shouldn't bother God with this.* Dear friend, if it is a concern to you, then it is a concern to God. If you're not absolutely sure you should be asking God for something, just ask yourself, *Is this something Christ would want to happen? Would Christ sign his name to this prayer I'm praying?* That's what Jesus meant when he said, "You may ask me for anything in my name, and I will do it" (John 14:14). Pray a prayer you believe he would agree with and be persistent.

In his second letter to Timothy, Paul wrote, "I have been reminded of your sincere faith, which first lived in your grandmother Lois and in your mother Eunice and, I am persuaded, now lives in you also" (1:5). In other words, Timothy's grandmother's faith had been passed on to him. This reminds us not just to pray

for this generation, but to pray down the generations, for our children, for their children, their children's children, and their mates.

We can make a difference in the future generations if we start praying now. Prayer isn't man's idea. God tells us to pray. Jesus, the very Son of God, prayed constantly. Prayer is at the heart of friendship with God, and prayer for our families is our responsibility and our privilege.

John Yates is rector of The Falls Church (Episcopal) in Falls Church, Virginia. Susan has written several books and is a frequent guest on *FamilyLife Today* and other national radio programs. They are popular speakers at marriage and family conferences around the country. Their five children (and their spouses) have joined them in writing this book about the family.